Falling Body

Falling Body

DAVID CAVANAGH

salmonpoetry

Published in 2009 by
Salmon Poetry
Cliffs of Moher, County Clare, Ireland
Website: www.salmonpoetry.com
Email: info@salmonpoetry.com

ISBN 978-1-903392-98-0

Cover artwork: *Coming Around*, oil painting by Gail Salzman
www.gailsalzman.com
Cover design & typesetting: Siobhán Hutson

For Sharon
and in memory of my brother, Ken

Acknowledgments

Many thanks to the editors of the following journals in which some of the poems in this book first appeared:

CANADA:
CV_2: contemporary verse 2, "Neil Armstrong Shoots the Moon"
The Dalhousie Review, "Distracted"
The Fiddlehead Review, "High Wire"
Grain, "At the Mercy," "CAD"
The Malahat Review, "Cut Cedar," "Whiffleball", "Waitress I Never Knew"

IRELAND:
The SHOp, "Quantum Jump," "Heart Attack in Wartime"
Southword, "Black Snow"

U.K.:
Agenda, "Never Mind"

U.S.A.:
Green Mountains Review, "Mission"
Seven Days, "The Wait"

Warm thanks to the other poets, friends, and family members who gave crucial support during the writing of this book. Special thanks to Jessie Lendennie and Siobhán Hutson of Salmon Poetry for their tireless efforts on behalf of poetry and so many poets, including me. My deep gratitude to Sharon Webster, Greg Delanty, and Aaron Thomas for their fine insights about the poems. Finally, special thanks to Richard Harrison for his caring, critical eye and for seeing, truly, the whole.

With each step you fall forward slightly.
And then catch yourself from falling.
Over and over, you're falling.
And then catching yourself from falling.
And this is how you can be walking and
falling at the same time.

LAURIE ANDERSON

Contents

Neil Armstrong Shoots the Moon

Neil Armstrong on his back deck
gazes up at the blatant moon
the way you might peer at a vacation photo
of Seattle propped on a cluttered
bookcase. Says, "I've been there." Or

Neil Armstrong shakes his bristled head,
"I've been THERE?" Same
as you, tossed in time, squint at all those
glossed Seattles floating
deep in inner space, far from your daily orbit.

Or even, like Neil, bathed in moondust,
feel the prick of small
skulking knowledge you've been there
but don't know the place
at all beyond a booted step on a crusty shell.

Or Neil says, "You know, I was only first
because I was sitting near
the door," and you recall a burbling phone
one tea-cozy morn,
all lunatic thereafter, a kettle whistling mad.

Or, if with a little launch of ego Neil says,
"I'VE been there," you wonder
what kind of "I" it was saw Seattle, and if
you still know that person
you know you badly need to know.

Or, less likely but to be hoped, Neil swivels
a craggy pate
up to the orange-yellow Buddha, feels
implausible rain or tears,
no telling which, kiss his runneled cheek.

Just as you, one ragged half-corked evening,
home in on the moonface
backlit in the bathroom mirror – so like
your father's, so much
stranger – gravely seeming to say,

"I've been watching
you for years. Time you noticed. Who
are you, really, what
is your intention, where have you been
to give off such a light?"

Black Snow

Straddling that smoky Tennessee walker,
Black Snow, just settled down for my
maiden ride, lovely leather and muscled
bulk of him beneath me, I let the unfamiliar
reins go slack. He lurches, my neck whips
back, Guatemalan cap flies off, I yank
too hard, he rears, lord I'm hanging on.
My wife shrieks, "You don't have to...."
"He's only a city boy," she pleads to my
Kentucky in-laws hooting by the fence,
which sets them howling more. Whatever

else at that dilated instant, I am more
myself than in the loose change of days.
A bit of Black Snow I am as well,
grand centaur self, and both of us
are something else again – melted,
molten ice, the force that moves us,
electric, arcing across time, we are
fused and we are fuse. We are
black snow in summer, by god,
and ass-up silly to boot – all in one
hoot-erupting lunge of hock and hoof.

At that instant seized and seismic,
bless me, father, hubris, hubris,
I don't care, I was there, right there,
terrified, laughing, and was not thrown.

CAD

The artery
is clogged. Not a river, not a boulevard, not the downtown
rush-hour
expressway. And not the heart. The heart is fine. Artery.
The LAD,
the doctor calls it. Left Anterior Descending. The LAD is blocked,
90% silted in
with plaque. Blood backed up at the narrow. Still there is essential
trickle,
the corpuscular cargo of O_2 struggling upstream toward the heart.
The muscle
gasps for it, an ache like no other, a hollowness, as if a room
lost all kilter,
walls caving and distending while everyone at the party keeps
talking small,
the words grow wan, indistinct, even as the din swells, bulges,
a confusion
of emptiness and pressure. You're desperate to leave but can't.

> Marianne gets off the bus; you
> rush to embrace and in her eye
> see a new and terrifying stillness,
> your love turned back. Stunned
> stupid, you begin to pant,
> try to hold onto yourself.

Doctor, you say,
I can't find words; the chest felt the way it did when she
cut me
out of her life at the station, and the buses kept pulling in,
driving away.

Angina pectoris.
Surely a Roman empress. Capable of anything. A team of clinical

New Englanders
goes to work, determined, unimpressed, kind in their way, relentlessly competent.
Intravenous nitro, heparin drip. Angioplasty and stent, in through the leg at the femoral
artery and up into the sacred chamber, balloon and a bit of chicken wire to widen
the channel. It's all done with cameras, all on TV. Everyone murmurs satisfaction,
then it's back to the room, wired, electrodes in five places. No more nitro. The LAD
is restored. Supposedly all is fine now, but for the pills to take for life
and some so-so odds about re-stenosis, scar tissue plugging up
the works again. If so, back to the cath lab for another roto-rooter job,
ream that baby out. Or else bypass, circumferential highway, crack open
the chest and graft a borrowed vein around the gum-up.

The lesson?
None that makes a difference. You eat the same, work out as always.
Genes did it, says the doc. In another time, he might have said the stars,
or destiny, or fate, your earlier life as a hawk. All we know is what builds up
builds up and can kill. The lore of the massive coronary, the big kahuna,
tsunami that slams the seawall to shards, washes you back to the deep. No knowing
how long the stent will work, or if. You live now with Coronary
Artery Disease. You have the CAD within you.

It was years before you could
go again to the station. You
wouldn't give that much
away. One by one the women
left in tears you couldn't cry.

Though you're supposed to feel grateful, and you do –
the plumbing
repaired, no big blow-out, no trip beyond – there's no denying
the CAD
has hold of the LAD. Something has been taken from the everyday,
a sureness
revealed now as bogus but endearing. Bravado. Gone. And something
added, a stutter
thought of what comes next. Loss of compass, magnetic pull you can't
quite read,
the needle of your days knocked off true north. Fear of exertion, too,
when often
it's the only thing that helps – onto the treadmill and work
up a sweat,
in every bead the unseen beat, alive, alive. You do well
to remember
it's not the heart. The heart is fine. Just fine.

Security

Take off
shoes.
Bundle
belongings
in gray plastic
bins. Place
on conveyor
to xray. Walk
thru gunmetal
doorframe
from one
room to the
same room.
Watch
uniformed
watchers
watching
electronic
displays.

Get taken
aside for
select
screening.
Place small
socked
feet inside
Sasquatch
prints on
rubber rug.
Spread arms
wide like
Da Vinci

drawing
with
protracted
circles.

Wonder
about crisp
blue-shirted
woman, silver
badge with
eagle, dark
wand that
traces you
in air. Feel
latexed,
intentional
hands pat
you down
all over.

Think about
how no one
seems to
mind much,
even you.
Think about
parting mono-
toned advice:
have a
pleasant
day. Think
about flight.

Mission

First, duct-tape the poem
to your torso. Pull on
a loose sweater. Make
sure nothing shows.
Walk steadily, head up,
into a crowded café,
church, bus terminal.
Slip one hand under
the fabric. Finger
the central image.
Test the line breaks,
the carefully fractured
rhythm. Check
the tension, the dark
ragged ending. Look
straight ahead but
take in the whole
room, every tic. Take
special note of clusters.
Look for loners, their
eyes. Think about
maximum impact.
Choose your moment.

At the Mercy

for Pat Cavanagh

This tender July evening, my brother in hospital
    with virulent strep from an insect bite
or yardwork scrape. Minding his own, then
    hijacked – jazzed-up, hooded bacteria
careen through his body, leave him like a gutted
    school bus in Gaza. Or a charred
hillside in coastal California – firestorm
    in the system, raging up leg into lymph
almost to the heart, ravaging as it goes, leaving
    behind a bloated limb and fever
blazing in a counter-burn, both fires racing
    for control of the vitals. Finally backed down
days later, antibiotic ten times the home dose
    dripping into the vein. Me miles away
on my porch, chest pains again, the artery
    wincing with worry, or sympathy, or disease,
or imagination, this attack out of the blue, fanatic
    bio-terror, savage, single-mindless, what
means, this limpid evening, the sinking sun
    bathing the alder Caravaggio-bright, west wind
rising, invisible, long *sshhh* in the shaken leaves.

Heart Attack in Wartime

Who knew the heart
        might break before it broke,
seize up like an old piston
        locked against its casing?
Just before that final insult, months

of bombs and bellicosity had worn
        me down, our human
face gone grim, gaunt with killing
        and, almost as bad, the truth
tortured nightly on the news
        till it gave in, said yes, kill
the bastards, they deserve it, they
        are not us, everywhere
in malls and kitchens they said
        yes, kill them now, even
Dorothy in Kansas said kill, kill….

Faith drains away. The heart loses
        heart. What kind
of leader orders people's slaughter?
        What kind of people follow,
the masses become mass murderers?
        The shame of wasted
nation's soul, Whitman's pride, all that
        generous, raucous energy
gone bad, fouled by self-interest, fear,
        meaning turned to meanness,
as if this US had seen its rich arterial
        blood thickened to sludge,
dammed up in the heartland, till heart itself
        drained, shuddered, stopped.

At the same, strange time you stirred
the larger heart in me.
Years after our first, loamy love, still
a flowering, still the tensile
stalk, still your eyes, their warm
regard, your small hands
that love the dirt, coax the green

from it. Never that private touch more
crucial or imperiled. This dying –
quite the shocker as I'm couched before
the peep show of far-away
war. So few things this final. If I had
again that thoughtless sparrow,
health, I'd rage against the hate and rip
the ideologues who live as if
stone dead, all rigoured up and righteous.

I'd wear it on my sleeve till
it wore out, scream blue
murder at the murderers, have a heart,
I'd say, have a bloody heart.
Or maybe not. That smell...lilac, bursts
so sudden, full, like velvet
drapery. My time is short. The treasure
of your imploring glance
I take with me; the sound of my own faltering
breath, full of the splendid
mystery; and memory, as long as it may last.

Moment

Look back and forward
    to this now.
Your parents yet unmet, your
    grave un-entered.
An electric wire hums, taut
    between then and then.

Cycle

The way a wheel turns,
    grounded
low, spinning free up top.
    A life like that,
you might get somewhere.

Waitress I Never Knew

Harelipped you were beautiful,
    loon-lonely eyes and lithe
shape split by the veering, renegade
    lip. Asymmetrical, utterly

stirring. After the surgery I wasn't
    even sure it was you, so nearly
regular your mouth, just a hint
    of up-pull, so flashing

your look. You seemed younger, less
    sad, less sure, too, as if you
had become your own little sister.
    How I wanted that wildly rising

line still to be there. I had no right.
    I know your life is better now,
hear it in the loose swing of your chatter.
    But your glance – more flit

than flash. Something has been smoothed
    away I loved. At least one self
wrenched from bed by thugs you never
    knew, hustled off, never seen

again. Now it is left to find out
    what was lost in that line
you were born with, what became
    of the disappeared, what grace

resides in that thin river you
    no longer have to cross,
and where it may be found again,
    and why I worry so.

Man Reading

inside the glass box framed with steel
that fronts the city parking lot,
9 years, 14,000 hours, $9.50 per,
no bennies, rocks back'n forth on a stool.

Reads like a sonnovabitch. Proust
is nothing to him, everything. No
worry about remembering things past.
He's a vault crammed with detail,
one of those impossible ships in a bottle

rigged with Nabokovs, Forsters, Faulkners,
9 years of pages flapping against head winds.
Or he is the bottle itself, stoppered,
beat-up, bobbing, ship of pages out to sea.
Or an installation, public art, "Man Reading,"

phenom in our time as the pre-occupied
pull up, lower a window, thrust a dollar. He
opens the slide, gives a glance, takes the bill,
pops the barrier, eyes already back to book.
They roll away. His plots pile up like seasons.

He is also a man from Highgate, 40 miles
north; 40 years old, lives with his ailing
mother in their clapboard village saltbox.
Four days a week drives south to the city,
takes his glassed-in perch, punches tickets,

reads the day, catches the drift of all that passes
in or out. Aquarium on wheels, he thinks,
as a Grand Marquis with stolid heads
floats past. Drinks coffee from a plaid plastic
thermos, smokes steadily, flat thumb, yellowed

forefinger turning the page inside the cloud
that fills the space, plumes out the window
slid open, slid shut. Glass tepee, he thinks,
smoke signals. Parking attendant,
he thinks, a comma, parking, attendant.

"Jeune Fille"

she softly says,
half smile, half
pout, as I shy
by. She's right,
she is, and is
for sale,
almost midnight
in the streaming
video of *la*
rue St. Denis.

Hot pants, sky
heels, late
teens. She lights
up, leans
toward co-
corner-worker,
laughs. Between

johns – guy
with pants
down to his knees
in the parked
car she just
sprang from,
dark side
street, good
dollar deed
done. Easy
laugh, snappy
as new
bills. Neon
behind her

a blazing
halo, hot
marquee.

Her *jeune*
fille opener
hangs there –
savvy come-on,
sure, but maybe
too a low-pitched
plea, subliminal
whimper she
can't yet hear
on rampant
St. Denis.

And me
rattled to
my middling
core on pavement
stained with
the old business
of baffled longing.
Le soir si jeune.

Whiffleball

Slices air, that bat—a whoosh, a crack, the white
whiffle line-drives clear across the lawn,
defies by greater force its whiffle-self,
does a sudden bottom-out and stutters
down to earth. Nine times in a row the woman
pounds the ball to field. A few
home runs away, the blue-grey ropey
St. Lawrence curls toward the sea. She's

no ball player, really; just seized
at the family picnic, screen-porched,
pinned to the wicker, the too familiar
chatter that started thin as gauze
soon battened to a complex quilt
of comfort stitched with compliance
draped heavy, stifling, over her.

She has to move. Strides past wrought-iron
chairs to the plate, right into the game, smack
among the men, the running, laughing men
and boys who wave her in; she takes
the stick, waits for the pitch, whacks the thing
nine times, whack, whack, whack, whacks
it for the watching one, the prozacked
TVed, pillowed one, whacks it for the battered
one, whacks it for the one with the literal
hole in her heart, smoke from the longest
possible cigarette curling up past her eyes,
whacks it for the one who left, ran north
across the river with a loaded U-Haul, just
before daybreak, just in time, just herself,
whacks it again for the empty chair, the one

to come. Turns, walks back, swings the porch
door wide, sits by the silent others. Some
nervous joking, nine hard cuts without a miss,
where'd you learn that, girl, the whiffle
biting the grass or sailing high, but whacked,
for sure; every woman there obscurely
pleased and wary both, knowing a line
has been drawn, a question asked, a window
sash shoved high; knowing they dare not
approach except with fluttery banter.
Whiffle talk. All she knows herself
for sure, the sound and shock of contact
running up the arms. Feels good, like a river,
inevitable, thick ropes of water moving on.

"You Need Not Be Present to Win"

But you do. You need
to buy a ticket and you
need to show up and you
need to be vulgar
about claiming the prize.
You need to learn
how to live with your
delight and you need
to find the bit of
raggedy grace still left to you
after all the losing tickets
crumpled, tossed, until today
these perfect digits the breezy
media blonde has briskly
plucked, as if it barely mattered,
one by one zeroing in on you –
reaching behind the particular,
briefly unlatched door
in the spinning plastic ball.

Distracted

Who knows why? Bamboozled by glare, shadows,
reflections (maybe even their own,
Narcissus lost in love), or crazy with spring
(Icarus winging free toward the sun),
or radar scrambled by too many cues, the waxwings
swoop full tilt into the bay window
of the children's library. Every spring they
thud against the safety glass
and break the heart of the librarian. After the first
few she can't take it, calls vets,
agencies, even 911, not noticing the number
is the same for rescue and terror.

(Those damned dead Greeks. Why bring them into
it? Why not?) Yesterday at the mall
a doorway I strode toward, only half regarding,
turned out to be a window.
Unlike the Red Sea that parted so graciously
for Moses, this see-through wall
bounced me like a tiresome drunk at the door
of a downtown bar. Not even
the drama of shattering glass, just a miniature
red sea opening above a startled eye.

The eye, of course, the problem. Distracted by
the splendidly worn jeans of the sales
woman bending over the display to my right,
I had thought myself in a miracle
so fine that all must open before it. Plate glass,
however, so good at transparency,
gives nothing away. Except suddenly I had her
undivided. Nothing like blood
on the loose to encourage a little focus.

Dripping bright red "sold" stickers onto her
hardwood floor, I politely
asked for a towel. She ran to call her boss
instead. Not my best come-on,
it seemed, though I had hoped the flow would
lend a certain Pollock-like intensity.
Truly I should know better at my age than
to ogle, except knowing has little
to do with it; usually it's done before the brain
has any say. Most likely genes led the way,
same as the poor waxwings. Genes or delusion,
some cock-eyed vision the world
could not accommodate. Or wouldn't. Like Icarus
or self-loverboy, none of us much
choice but to play the play and wing headlong.

Blood, as so often, the result. My mishap silly,
theirs catastrophic; 20 or more,
one by one they drive their black-masked
heads into the invisible
pane. Drunk on fallen berries, maybe. Eden
gone mad. Anyway, they're down.
Why rankles – unseen ache behind a cross-stitched
brow. No telling, really. None.

Optic Nerve

As I've said, or implied, or dreamed maybe,
 yes, a thing of REM flashing
red like taillights in and out of sight on hills,
 we need to pay attention.

Focus, see what's behind the mirror,
 the dazzle, the days,
the mute front door, the household patterns,
 partner, patter, grocery
trip, behind the tax burden, the *laissez-faire*,
 the boxed blue eye. In

my case, scarred retina, minute adhesions
 making blur, akin to floaters.
Ideopoathic. No idea where my scars come from.
 My family no different
from yours. All I know, my verticals wriggle
 like a highway on a searing
afternoon, then straighten at the edge of vision.
 Wooly ball in the middle.
I've made a life out of the corner of the eye.
 Head-on seemed too hard,
mean moguls shifting in shadow and glare.

 I always thought myself
a private investigator, my blindnesses my own.
 Now I begin to suspect
I'm a very public eye. *Dick publique, c'est moi*;
 my card, *s'il vous plaît*, take.
My floaters just versions of your own dark
 quavers, passing lunar
eclipses, black bubbles of the soul. But screw

this cool palaver. Time to pay
sharp heed to all our wavy lines. Start here:

Why did you leave
right after dinner that evening we seemed ready
to make love? Or was I
the one who left? And is it a difference
that makes a difference
now, at the fuzzy centre where we move?

High Wire

"To live is to be on the wire. Everything else is just waiting."
KARL WALLENDA

What the hell, says Karl, back on the wire
after the fall
in Detroit – magic of the 7-man pyramid
meeting concrete
circus floor, two cousins dead he'd
led into the trade,
his own pelvis crushed and badly healed.
Back on the wire, toes
curled around cable, calves taut as gut,
he walks, believing himself

alive. If his hands on the balancing pole aren't
loose & sensitive
as a polygraph, he'll never make it. Tiny
uncounted adjustments,
tips out there 12 feet either side of the wire,
dipping & hiking
like a hungry goldfinch with each millimeter
shift of his palms.
If he thinks too much he's a goner, thousands
in the stadium below
gasping his last huzzah. One word for it
only or he'll slip

hit the wire and, silent as a goblet, drop.
One word he won't
even say, barely even think, so distracting
the language, silly
at this gusty height. He moves like mercury,
deliberate, pure,

no sign of the tidal roar in his brain, whoosh
        that he craves
& could blow him free of the mindless
        coil; a simple word
he can't avoid or afford or deny: attend.

Never Mind

for Lillian Farrell

At 92, in and out, mostly out. Wind
        gusting through
that stuck open window, flowered
        curtain flapping.
"A nice man, eh!" (meaning my brother).
        Glance layered with
love and complicity. Then gone. Shade
        drawn down tight.

"My sweet Bernie." Fifty-two years
        her nephew, first I've
heard of Bernie, sweet or un-. Her mind
        in increments
washing back to sea; in bits returning,
        long-ago wreckage
whorled up and shored. Her spirit,

bright beacon with almost a century's
        sweep, sputters,
flares, goes dark. Blinks again at some
        recall, blanks,
blinks – yellow light on an unseen timer.

I visit 20 minutes. For her, an eon or
        an instant. Free of time,
trapped in it. I say I'll come back soon.
        Pretending it means.
"I love you," she says. "Always have."

Linked eyes. Both of us cheered by that
        "always," a sliver
of history, awareness of history, we hold,
        for a flicker, between us.

Dear Lillian

With your dying such a trump
    you've played.
The rest of us shuffling
    over and over,
trying to change the luck.

Cauldron of the Morn

Oatmeal, headed up by orange juice, caboosed
by coffee. A pleasant gathering of steam.
Same mealy gruel I loathed as a child and, oddly
now, enjoy. Same impossibly cheerful quaker
on the box, ruddy with faith and industry.
We called it porridge. Poor-idge. Mortar
for the ribs and soul. Stop up the cracks
against winter and all things venal or weak.
No coffee back then, but a dollop of cod liver
oil poured like a shot of the worst ever
whisky into the o.j. Blobbed back up top,
half-inch of oil slick after the spill. The o.j.,
my one bright hope in that repast, fouled.
But not to be ignored. Healthy, hated, endlessly
protested and mocked. Then down the subdued hatch
after mom laid down the law, so mysterious
its source and so powerful for that. Poor ma,
who insisted, against all abuse that grew stronger
as we did, and knew, I hope, as we almost knew
somewhere back of the whiny cake hole, how much
grit and caring and who knows what it took, decades
before gurus of low lipids and omega-3s chanted
smuggy mantras of oats and fish oil, day after
frigid day to boil that very non-instant brew,
morn after bleary winter morn to stir and serve up that pot of future.

Colours of the Heart

Black for the armbands grandpa wore
        to hoist up his shirtsleeves.
White for those sleeves, billowy,
        as he flapped his arms
and rounded the dining table. Maple
        the family table, a hay field
he circled, gathering speed – plane
        or old lost heron revving for takeoff.
Red for the snowsuit I was stuffed
        into, trundled outdoors,
charcoal the crusted old snow
        in our yard. What colour
the ache, opaque, muffled yell
        in his arm? Wine the couch
they laid him on, tawny the rug, blue
        my eyes wide and his lips,
grey his slackened jaw, the windowed sky.

Cyrus

dead at 47

"Cells live, cells die,"
he said. "It's not
complicated."

The biologist,
expert on
rare mosses
and the blind,
tenacious
life of spores,
speaking of his own
cellular riot, the burnt
out shell of self
to come, the plain
pine box he wanted,
no embalming
to interfere
with the slow
certain transmigration
back to earth.

Proving beyond
a mirror's doubt
how wrong
he had been
while right,
how deeply
complicated
it all (always)
is.

The Wait

after Lawrence Ferlinghetti

New Year's Eve, waiting for the ball to drop
        again. Waiting for the dancing
to begin, the band to wail like it has no choice.
        It has no choice.

I'm waiting for the woman in red shoes to move
        her sinuous self my way
and smile. I'm waiting for the stores to close.
        I'm waiting for one of the football guys
huddled over beers in the raucous bar to say, wait,
        what would T.S. Eliot say about that?
I'm waiting for the young woman showing serious
        cleavage to think about it.
I'm waiting for myself to stop. New Year's
        Eve, waiting for a storm,
the evening's tinsel to peel back and the innards
        of a year to be revealed.

My car is layered with salt. I'm waiting to wash
        it in the freezing air and turn the shell
to ice. I'm waiting for spring to start tomorrow
        and the moon to take over.

I'm waiting for pro hockey players to take up
        knitting, and knitters to bristle
over politics. I'm waiting for the president
        to be one. I'm waiting for a job
to be more than that, and to be no more than it
        should be. I'm waiting for America
to grow weary of money and move on. I'm
        waiting for cell phones to yield
to conversation. I'm waiting for the prisons
        to be opened so we can meet

the million we think are not like us. I'm waiting
        for dinner with the Chinese woman
who made my shoes and shirt. I'm waiting for comfort
        to remove its anaesthetic needle
from my brain. I'm waiting for comfort to blush
        with shame and confusion,
to wonder why it finds itself so uncomfortable.

New Year's Eve and I'm waiting for some words
        to jump the barbed wire and throw off
their orange jumpsuits: liberal, feminist, intellect –
        dangerous felons all. I'm waiting
for grade schools to embrace children and lock up
        the tools of control, instead of all that
vice versa. I'm waiting for some intelligent design.
        I'm waiting for the body to howl
and the spirit to listen. New Year's Eve and I'm
        waiting for the war to be fought
with razor-sharp love, waiting for the battle to turn
        inner. I'm waiting for the troops
to come home and tear the little yellow magnets
        off our cars, say you call that
support? Say to hell with support. What's needed
        now – Sinatra knew it, sing it again,
Frank, why not – what's needed now is all of us.

New Year's Eve and I remember now the ball
        has been well and truly dropped,
again and again the fireworks splayed against
        the played out sky. What becomes
of that spinning globe each year after its midnight
        fall? We hardly know. Now
I'm waiting for the ball to rise and silent rockets
        spray the sky with colour
beyond all telling. I'm waiting for the dancing,
        and the music to be heard.

Sorry We Are

In Victoria, city of lights and ancient flora,
huge buses with the broad faces of totems
crawl by flashing digitized confession:
"SORRY I AM"

Giant Yodas of urban transit they are,
lost apologetic mammoths. Queenly
city, hungry we are for your destinations,
and sorry for your buses' sorrow.
Our own it is.

The next flash: "NOT IN SERVICE." Sad
but fair enough. We understand your woe. So
much history to traverse, so much paved over
that may not be unearthed, time there is
not enough.

Wood Voices

1

You cannot know
the ways of trees,
our burrowed cravings,
coded rings behind
gnarled defenses.
You only see green,
our laughing
in breezes, graceful
godward stretch.

Do not be deceived.
We are double
agents, carry
messages in cones,
bow with suspicion,
speak up only
in loud windstorms,
root in deepest
earth. Our needs
are not yours.

2

If you want to live here
you must obey
the silent law
of bullet. Your head
must be gun.

3

Stripped raw
by struggle.
More and more
the naked branch.
Emaciated women,
bloated men –
comrades way
too late. It's
always November
now. One
thin hope, deep
winter's long
indifferent
burn. Where
are the children?

Quantum Jump

for Sean Cavanagh

The wave that crashes
on the rocks
is made of particles that behave
so much like waves
the scientists
scratch their individual
heads until
they're one bobbing mass
and their
voices rise like spray.

~

Certain uncertain certainly
we are all
going to die one
day probably
is about all with precision
we can say.
No one has ever
not done it,
and I don't aim to be
the first.
Not that I lack
ambition,
only that aiming
doesn't
seem to help.

~

Still, smack the tennis
ball against
the wall often enough,
it could
one time go straight through.
So I say unto
you, phone the woman,
plant the rare
hibiscus. Most likely it
won't take,
except when it does.

What matters simply

against the downtown din is, simply, all
that matters. A whole life, as far as it goes
and has gone to get here. I'm talking now
about choice. Half a century of letting be
what will be, k-sera-ing my Buddhist butt around.

I'm here now in traffic to choose, to get on
with a certain wry amount of self. The burble
of a pigeon I can't see makes itself
part of the picture. In a land of distraction, pointing
is of the utmost. I don't care if it's hackeysack

you play, I admire the hours you took
to learn that soft-toed kick and the way you bend
to pick, again, the bag up off the ground.
Every act of faith seems absurd to those who lack
belief. If I can't play now when?

Black Iris

Buds of black iris tight as jars. What
 is left to sing about?
In the story of Icarus and Daedalus,
 I would have been dad:
respect for the sky and sea, don't dare
 fly too high. We know
what happened to the lad. Lived large,
 flew high, died into myth.

What can be said for D? Built the labyrinth
 as Minos asked, then pissed him off,
got tossed into his own maze. Soon figured
 to fly off,
ingenious with wax and feathers.
 Day done, he'd lost the boy.

Reckless on the wing, like a kid who
 gets his father's car first time
and feels the wind, the lad put the pedal
 down. Or was he stung
by genius in the air, no choice but strain
 straight at eternal fire?

What of life after feathers met the sea? If
 D ever smiled or flew
again, I'd like to know it now. Sip my coffee.
 Rain falls hard, steady, 5 a.m.,
before most people have any idea.

Without the boy we might not know of dad.
        Earth is nourished. Black iris,
                mostly blue, really,
deepest indigo inside, tender and proud
        as a bruise, opens
to the sky, shows glory part of a week,
                then dies. The plant
lives on. Leaves carve upward like spears.

No Child Except the Air

No seed of mine
has sprouted in the usual way of men.
No kids cradled, no toddlers
scoot across playgrounds, no teenagers
dangle in doorways for car keys.
All I've done, breathe the best I could,
read the inhaled currents,
give the changed air back to itself – some old
scheme I barely understand.
Serene trees abracadabra dioxide back into O_2.
Then down into the lung's
dark forest, out along the thin red rivers
of the body's heartland,
peninsulas. And so on, inspiration, ex-,
life's essential gases
forth and to. Am I child or parent? What I take
I give and what I give
I'm given back. Flummoxed by this planetary
magic and my need.

I love. I run away. I hold my breath, then notice,
then pant like a kid
late for the game. I read a book on how to breathe.
Imagine! Then, thank gods,
there's you, my love, my atmospheric *sensei*.
You teach me
how to take it in. I mimic your attentiveness,
try to give it back.
If I can post my longing somehow on the air,
I may one day say
satisfied. Sounds grand. Heads-up heartfelt
practice is the plan.
Hold, let go. Yearn and walk away. Keep

breathing. A boy with red
backpack ambles past – someone I don't know,
or know no longer, or not
yet, and yet inhabit. I call out, hey, good gait.
A look back. Wonder.
Too late for some things, not for others. I breathe
his future; he breathes mine.

Waking

Slanty light, shivery leaves.
Wind, and the way you see
things. Legs curled
on the sofa, flannel pjs,
over-sized coffee
cupped in two hands.
Slowly you unfurl
white wings of longing
along the branching day.

Bended Knee

Christmas morn, by the spangled tree,
when I moved in you – urgently
awkward on the recliner – both of us
laughing & excited – like fast
water over pebbles – the Messiah
knew it had been born,
and all the shepherds knelt.

Cut Cedar

Near the end of a stuffed-up,
  slung-low, head cold day,
a couple of excellent blisters
      from clipping
  the irrepressible cedars
that line the grassy drive.

    Index finger and palm
bubbled raw with hacking.
 Now I can barely hold
the pencil that tries
   to get it down. So

lucky, this pain reminds,
  the chafe and sweat,
    the forearm ache,
the old growth scent of redwood
      cut up close. Grant

    me, please, the sense
to take it all, always, in.
 My greatest fear,
   to be a thoughtless blade
or nerve-dead limb.

   Never stop rubbing me
      raw, red, tender –
nostrils smart with sharp
  familiar longing — enough
to feel this odd, this blessedly
    shaky in the telling.

Meta-Morning

Every morning the *moi*
staggers out of dream.
Within minutes
it clamours for the stage.
Bathroom spotlights, mirror
monitor, the mewling
song begins: I, I, I.

Just try to stay out of it.
Shave.
The day may have something
to say.

~

The shy air
of pre-dawn
surprises your
neck as you
step off the stoop.
The long lovely
travail of walking
when you think
you know the end
of all walking. Try
not to make it mean.

~

Stuck in the car behind
the yellow Bluebird
school bus, I'm STOP-
signed and red-flashered

at every farmhouse.
Human nestlings
trail down the driveway
up into the box. Shadows
move in the aisle, then
settle. Eggs
safe in their carton.
I might as well be in reverse.
Late for work again.

~

If you sit still long
enough, everything you
haven't thought of
begins to move
across a screen
you didn't know
was there.
A marigold
the size of a fist
glistens, drips
rivulets of rain
along the hand
that holds it. Now's
the chance to slow-dance
with essentials. Don't
breathe a word.

Falling Body

Falling Body

You look like a man who has had procedures.
        Well, yes. And you?

Come out from behind the curtain. The mirror
        and the mirror's mirror waiting.

~

High over city centre, Mount Royal's cross still
        seems unfinished, like scaffolding

or a ruin, an undone. At night it stars,
        an electric saviour to guide

a yearned landing or ward off swooping danger.
        The city throbs below.

~

My Montreal beats on. The hookers strut.
        The diners dine. Fine

neighbourhoods wind uphill, gather gracefully
        beneath the silent cross.

A respectful distance made of trees. The cemetery
        slopes like a beret

down the mountain's other side. Thousands of marble
        crosses Jones-ing the big one.

        Ring around the rosey,
        Pocketful of posies.

Ashes, ashes,
We all fall down.

~

"What's it all about?" is a question with heft.
It's all about gravity. And lift-off.

"I've fallen for you" is a top-flight biblical come-on.
It means, "You send me to the moon."

It means, "I'm in orbit." It means, "I'd climb up
on the cross for you." You with shapely

everything, esp. what's behind those astonishing
green eyes that laugh me off.

Could use a cold meteor shower about now.
Rain down on my need.

~

Horribly buckled old woman by the Royal Vic
hospital door. Rankled as a cat,

she waves me off hard when I hold it open.
How upright is that!

A bit stooped myself. I wear my Montreal
uneasily. All those flagrant

syllables. Cloak of ages. So much hidden
by what's revealed.

~

A man who's had heart bypass is suspect.
        He'll say anything to hear

the beat. He'll say anything to get it off
        his chest. He's a wishbone

sawed precisely in two and wired back together
        for another go. No longer

any question whether wishes come true. They all
        do except the ones that don't.

~

He's in freefall as long as he believes it. Spreads
        his arms and legs, becomes a star,

thinks large about things tiny. Slows way down.
        Others plummet past,

bits of complex debris in a grim yank to hit ground
        running. Still, it all feels

like a gift from a heart that has cooled, stopped,
        warmed, started up again.

~

Breathe into the machine. So many gizmos
        to take one's vitals. His favourite:

the oxygen meter clothespegged onto his index
        finger. Adam & God in the creation

painting tending grandly toward each other.
        Robust naked limbs stretch

across the cosmos, Adam languid, God
        straining to make it

happen. Almost understanding. Michelangelo
        fingertips the mystery.

~

Whispered in the theatre: If it gets really bad,
        you can always take a dive

from the balcony seat, swan out over the crowd.
        Acceleration: 32 feet

per second per second. The law of falling bodies.
        Whispered back:

That beats all! It's the per second per second
        that kills me.

~

Baby sparrow toddles on concrete by the brick
        office building. Tweets

non-stop after its tumble. No sign of nesting
        mom. What now?

~

He knows from what he knows of what his nephew
        said of quantum physics

that all he can know is that he has a tendency
        to exist. A lesson he'd like

to hang onto but finds a little tidy for the ram-
    bunctious air near earth.

He loves the tendencies. The ripple through him
    when a certain woman laughs,

as if a room changed colour instantly, pale
    blue blooming to saffron,

and if a room, why not a continent, a constellation?
    Pleiades, sisters, saviours.

~

Awe, cool. Desire, hot. The mix, exquisite squirm.
    I've never been to San Francisco

but listening to Tony Bennett I think maybe I left
    my heart there, too. Explains

a lot. I thought it was broken in Montreal. Re-birthed
    & re-routed on the shores

of Lake Champlain. Like Samuel plying the waterway
    unnamed in 1609, I'm on a liquid

border, sailing virgin territory ringed by untouched
    fir. At my age, hallelujah.

~

I mean simply that the streets are hot with swagger.
    The boat has left that I am on.

Yearn. A wayward star, I fall and burn for thee.
    In love with this raucous

atmosphere, faster, falling. The frontier
        beckons. So green.

~

Gangly young Goth with pierced bellybuttonnose
        eareyebrow and tattooed

everythingelse stalks the scene on Church St. Flirts
        darkly with a fishnetted lass.

How to make love in jackboots is the hope
        and hurt of the day.

~

Newspaper thuds onto the porch. Broken
        word of the broken world

tubed tight in an orange wrapper. Pipe
        bomb or prison jumpsuit.

What to think? Not in my backyard. Better
        left unsaid.

~

Ordnance is a military word – means blood & bone
        not where they're supposed to be.

Iraq falls down on its knees, weeps toward Mecca.
        More ordnance is the answer

from the sky. The torn child by the pillar writes
        furiously into the future.

~

History will record that the U.S., forced to adopt
fundamentalist Islam

as the state religion, found it not so different,
really, from the old one.

About the *Koran*, it was said: We didn't read
the *Bible* either. Allah Allah in free.

~

It took 100,000 years for us to hold hands
and walk downtown together.

Tell Michelangelo he can come down now
from the ceiling. Earth ain't

so bad, except. In 1860 a man could beat
his wife and kids with a stick

no thicker than his thumb. In English Common
Law they called it

the Rule of Thumb; they called it progress.

Little Jack Horner sat in the corner
eating his Christmas pie.
He put in his thumb & pulled out a plum
and said ooh what a good boy am I.

Fingers in the pie again, eh Jack! It's the stick
for you, Jack. The stick for you.

~

With my ear on your belly I feel an ocean's
fall and rise, hear the base drum

rhythm at the core. My fingers trace your thigh,
ridge line of my horizon.

~

Aunt Lillian in her 60s fell and broke her femur,
or her femur broke and

she fell. No one knows. A dervishy problem,
cause and effect. Better

to acknowledge simply we have a fall, we have
a broken femur, and before that,

movement. Lillian found it hard to move on.
Other things got broken

that day. Fear bloomed ever after. A soul gone
white and shaky that was wild.

~

I've been avoiding the issue of Adam-and-Eve.
They chomp an apple

and the rest of us have to work like hell whole
lives, not to mention

plagues, quakes, wars, you name it. The original
family madness. Stupid pluckers.

~

All the king's horses and all the king's men
Couldn't put Humpty together again.

After my first bike pitched me head over handlebars,
I woke up walking with mom,

an ugly plum ripening on my forehead. Things
were never the same.

Couldn't wait to get back on the bike and wander
strange neighbourhoods,

streets opening like thighs. Something about
concussion that intoxicates.

The beauty of jagged memory. The gritty, luscious
work of retrieval.

~

St. Brendan's Church in Rosemont is an upside down
boat. Curved ribs of the hull

vault toward God. Sundays the boy walked 2 miles
to sit beneath its arch

at Mass. Like those Irish he'd never heard of,
heaving the *curragh*

down the beach, turtle hauling its shell to sea.
Small in the pew, he had no idea.

Drunk with incense, crescendos of pipe organ,
daydream of Miss DiStefano,

grade 2 teacher of mischief and wisdom, divine
        legs tucked under her desk.

Alone in the island city called home, fishing
        for signs he didn't know

he was fishing for. The boat was beautiful.
        The boat was upside down.

~

Christ down for the 3rd time, at the 9th station
        buckling under the tree

he'd be nailed to. Bent on cleaning up
        after Adam-and-Eve.

He bled like any innocent. He bled like an Iraqi,
        till he didn't. Three days

later, Resurrection. Up an' at 'em. Mission,
        one might have said,

accomplished. Except for a problem with staff
        assignments. Peter, the Rock

upon which He built, was crucified upside down.
        Then 2 millennia of spectacular

evil, hate, bumbling. Peter Piper's pickled. Right
        side up in the back pew the kid

blinks like a canary. A holy cage, mahogany mine,
        groaning wooden beams upflung.

~

Did Jesus note the instant his heart halted? And did
he die because it stopped,

or did it stop because his heart was broken? It was
a sacred muscle; that much

we know. The rest is tendency, quantum leaps &
ballyhooed second comings.

Much to be learned from a broken bone, even
more, perhaps, from death,

though who remains to do the learning is
an open question.

~

Brendan the navigator set sail from Ireland,
6th c. seeking the Promised Land

in a leather boat. The world was a plate.
Iceland, Greenland, New-

foundland. Some say he tagged them all.
Then why not Montreal,

a boat upturned and planted, hull to the wind,
an odd-job steeple added,

the keel it never had. A prayer for lost sailors
in Montreal, a boy

drawn in by 15 centuries of awe, a candle lit
by loneliness, his dime.

~

The 10-year old wheels a long time on his bike,
        sun-hazy streets of Rosemont-

Hochelaga leading him like Champlain's rivers.
        Overlook: Angus train yards,

a tangle of tracks, spurs, shunts, and block-long
        machine sheds where thousands

hammered & hauled. More tracks than a mind
        might manage – an intern's

binge of stitches, manic sheet music, cross-
        hatched message he has

no clue. Hard and gleaming, the rails stream
        importantly out of sight.

He squints through sweat, what he knows and
        now knows he doesn't

know, filling him, chest out, chest in, regular
        rise and fall, release.

~

From inside a high hospital window a pale
        frail man views the cityscape

for almost the last time. Black limbs of alder,
        maple, poplar stark against

corn snow, the slick black streets tail-lit
        all the way to the great river,

thick dark braid around his island. Beyond,
        the hills of south shore,

blue and brooding, fade. Long silence. Then,
"Fantastic." Is all

my father says. His torch-eyes sweep my way,
turn back. I'm burned sad, glad.

~

Chunks of quarried marble ring the 90-foot
deep pool. Vermont. A palisade

of gleaming birches. Thousand-pound shards
tilt up, all angles, as if

a giant sculptor had given up, stalked off. A man
made of wrinkles

emerges from leaves on a rusty old Raleigh,
glides to the edge where stone

becomes black water. I watch him strip naked,
pad onto blazing bright

slab cantilevered – a gangplank or wing – out
over the shimmery dark. V's

his arms upward. Bunches himself and swans
through air, slices down in.

Pops up among wavelets, climbs out, re-dresses,
rides away again into the woods.

We all fall down. So what, says the birch.
Ashen limbs meet the sky.